W...

01

NORTH YORK MOORS

BOOK THREE - NORTHERN MOORS
Eskdale and the Coast

C000170788

HILLSIDE GUIDES

FREEDOM OF THE DALES
40 selected walks
Full colour hardback

80 DALES WALKS
Omnibus edition of Books 4,6,8,11 and (in part) 10,21
Published by Cordee, Leicester

WALKS
ON THE
NORTH YORK MOORS
BOOK THREE – NORTHERN
Eskdale and the Coast

by

Paul Hannon

HILLSIDE PUBLICATIONS

HILLSIDE PUBLICATIONS
11 Nessfield Grove
Exley Head
Keighley
West Yorkshire
BD22 6NU

First published 1988
3rd (Revised) impression 1993

Page 1 illustration:
Beggar's Bridge, Glaisdale

The maps in this book are based upon
the 1914-1930 Ordnance Survey 1:10,560 maps

ISBN 1 870141 20 2

Printed in Great Britain by
Carnmor Print and Design
95/97 London Road
Preston
Lancashire
PR1 4BA

INTRODUCTION

THE NORTH YORK MOORS NATIONAL PARK

The North York Moors is the fourth largest of our ten National Parks, designated in 1952 with an area of 553 square miles. It is probably the best-defined upland area of all, rising island-like from the surrounding countryside. This creates an impression of much greater altitude than its very modest summit of 1490 feet attains. If asked which of the Parks is bottom of the height table, few would be likely to provide the correct answer, the North York Moors.

To the north is the Cleveland Plain, westwards the Vales of Mowbray and York, and southwards the Vale of Pickering while to the east is the ultimate low point, the North Sea. The Park itself however has a solid upland mass spreading from the centre towards the western escarpments, where one can walk for mile upon mile and lose little altitude. It is of course all this heather-clad moorland for which the National Park is best known, for there is no similar expanse anywhere else in the country.

Heather moors, despite their profusion, are only one aspect of this diverse region, for here are some delightful green valleys and a spectacular length of coastline composed largely of rugged cliffs. There are sandy shorelines and rocky coves, and inland some shapely summits, fascinating rock outcrops, beautiful waterfalls, and despite all the forestry some enchanting indigenous woods remain. The hand of man has been everywhere, even on the lonely moortops which are littered with ancient burial mounds and standing stones. The scores of villages range from fishing ports to moorland farming communities, though many of the villages are to be found beneath the hills, taking advantage of their shelter.

Man has also left ruined abbeys and castles; some old roads including a drovers' route, a Roman road and numerous paved trods; absorbing relics of the former ironstone, alum and jet industries; and not least of all an unrivalled collection of wayside crosses, some being ancient Christian symbols, and others serving as waymarks or boundary stones.

This is walkers territory par excellence, with a plethora of long-distance and challenge walks crossing it. Best known are the first, the poor old Lyke Wake Walk, and the longest and best, the Cleveland Way.

The three titles in this series of guides cover the whole of the National Park, and are divided into three necessarily arbitrary but nevertheless well-defined areas.

THE ROAD NETWORK

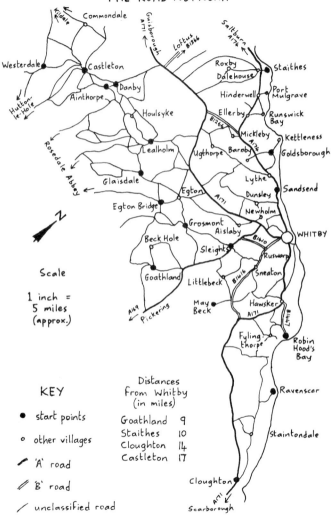

Scale

1 inch =
5 miles
(approx.)

KEY

- ● start points
- ○ other villages
- ╱ 'A' road
- ⫽ 'B' road
- ╱ unclassified road

Distances
from Whitby
(in miles)

Goathland   9
Staithes   10
Cloughton   14
Castleton   17

THE NORTHERN MOORS

The subject of this volume is the northern area of the Park, which is divided into two very distinct sections, namely Eskdale and its side-valleys, and the coastline and its environs. The Esk is the major river of the National Park, and this renowned salmon river is the only one which flows east to the coast. It rises on the highest moorland and retains its guardian moors almost to the sea. Its many tributaries are all arranged along its southern flanks, and include Westerdale (the proper head of Eskdale), Danby Dale, the Fryup Dales, Glaisdale and the valleys of the Murk Esk and Little Beck.

These dales are all fairly short in length, with only that of the Murk Esk containing a sizeable village. The main valley, however, makes up for this with characterful villages strung along its length, many of them serving as gateways to the side-valleys. A rare feature today is the presence of a railway station in almost every village, with the Esk Valley line providing the best method of travel in a valley where roads are narrow, winding and often steep.

Both the Esk and its railway terminate at Whitby, an absorbing coastal town which necessitates the only break in the Park's seaward boundary. To north and south the cliffs rise dramatically and support numerous villages. Some stand on the windswept clifftops, while the old fishing villages take advantage of the gaps to tumble down to the shore.

USING THIS GUIDE

Described in this book are 18 walks ranging in length from 3¾ to 7½ miles. With an average distance of 6 miles, they are ideally suited to half-day rambles. All are circular and begin from either a car park or a sensible parking location. Each of the walks has its own chapter, made easy to find by its number at the top corner of the page. Each chapter comprises of an 'immediate impression' diagram, detailed narrative and strip-map, and notes and illustrations of features of interest.

Although the strip-maps illustrating each walk should guide one safely around, they show nothing of the surrounding countryside, and for this purpose an Ordnance Survey map is to be recommended. The 1-inch Tourist map covers the entire park, and is therefore the perfect companion. Better still, there are two 1:25,000 Outdoor Leisure maps covering the whole area, with which one can plot or amend any route as necessary.

7

	Accommodation	Inn	Car park	Bus service	Rail station	Post office	other shop	Payphone	WC
Ainthorpe	•	•						•	
Beck Hole	•	•					•	•	
Botton			•			•	•	•	
Castleton	•	•	•	•	•	•	•		•
Cloughton	•	•	•			•	•	•	
Commondale	•	•			•	•		•	•
Dalehouse	•	•							
Danby	•	•	•	•	•	•		•	•
Egton Bridge	•	•	•	•		•		•	•
Glaisdale	•	•	•	•		•	•	•	•
Goathland	•	•	•	•	•	•	•	•	•
Goldsborough		•						•	
Grosmont	•	•	•		•	•		•	•
Hayburn Wyke	•	•		•					
Hinderwell	•	•		•		•	•	•	•
Lealholm	•	•	•		•	•	•	•	•
Littlebeck	•		•					•	
Lythe	•	•	•	•		•	•		
May Beck			•						
Port Mulgrave	•	•						•	
Ravenscar	•	•	•			•	•	•	•
Robin Hood's Bay	•	•	•	•		•	•	•	•
Runswick	•	•	•	•			•	•	
Sandsend	•	•	•			•	•		•
Sleights	•	•	•	•	•	•	•	•	•
Staithes	•	•	•	•		•	•	•	•
Westerdale	•					•		•	•

All known details are listed for the places visited on the walks. There are youth hostels at Westerdale, Wheeldale, Boggle Hole, Whitby, Saltburn and Scarborough. The last three are towns outside the National Park, and provide all services, as does Guisborough.

This is a general guide only.

SOME USEFUL ADDRESSES

Ramblers' Association
    1/5 Wandsworth Road, London SW8 2XX
        Tel. 071-582 6878

Youth Hostels Association
    Trevelyan House, St. Albans, Herts. AL1 2DY
        Tel. St. Albans (0727) 55215

North York Moors National Park Information Service
    The Old Vicarage, Bondgate, Helmsley, York YO6 5BP
        Tel. Helmsley (0439) 70657

The Moors Centre (National Park Visitor Centre)
    Danby, Whitby, North Yorkshire YO21 2NB
        Tel. Castleton (0287) 60654

Ravenscar National Trust Coastal Centre
    Ravenscar, Scarborough, N. Yorkshire YO13 0NA
        Tel. Scarborough (0723) 870138

Whitby Tourist Information Centre
    New Quay Road, Whitby, North Yorkshire
        Tel. Whitby (0947) 602674

North Yorkshire Moors Railway
    Pickering Station, Pickering, N. Yorks. YO18 7AJ
        Tel. Pickering (0751) 72508
        Talking Timetable 73535

British Rail - Passenger Enquiries (Esk Valley Line)
    Tel. Middlesbrough (0642) 243208

Tees and District Transport Company
    Newport Road Bus Station, Middlesbrough TS1 5AH
        Tel. Middlesbrough (0642) 210131

United Automobile Services
    Grange Road, Darlington, Co. Durham DL1 5NL
        Tel. Darlington (0325) 468771

'Moors Connection' Transport Guide
    % Elmtree Press and Publications,
    The Elms, Exelby, Bedale, North Yorkshire DL8 2HD
        Tel. 0677 - 424298

9

THE WALKS

Listed below are the 18 walks described, the walk number being the key to easy location in the guide

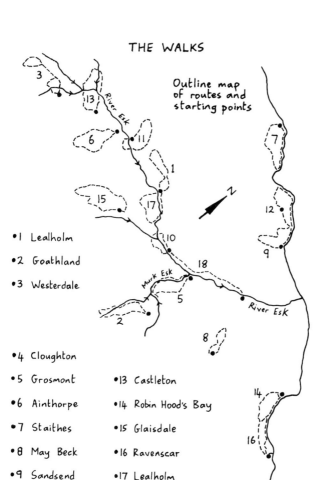

THE WALKS

Outline map of routes and starting points

N

River Esk

Murk Esk

River Esk

- 1 Lealholm
- 2 Goathland
- 3 Westerdale

- 4 Cloughton
- 5 Grosmont
- 6 Ainthorpe
- 7 Staithes
- 8 May Beck
- 9 Sandsend
- 10 Egton Bridge
- 11 Danby
- 12 Goldsborough

- 13 Castleton
- 14 Robin Hood's Bay
- 15 Glaisdale
- 16 Ravenscar
- 17 Lealholm
- 18 Sleights

WALK 1

DANBY BEACON AND LEALHOLM MOOR

6¼ miles

from Lealholm

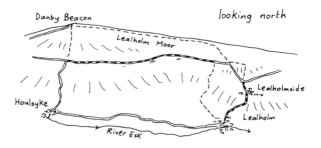

Largely straightforward walking
over or alongside open moorland,
visiting a renowned viewpoint

Use the car park
in the centre of
the village

THE WALK

From the village centre take the Danby/Castleton
road branching off from the junction just above the bridge,
but leave it almost immediately by a track up the near side
of the post office. At the top is a gate from where the
railway line is crossed. Turn left to the old station building
then up to a gate on the right, from where a green track
rises up through bracken. After dropping to cross a beck the
track is vacated half-way up the slope behind, along a much
pleasanter green track to the left. This rises steadily to
merge with a farm road before joining a moor road.

Turn left along the road with its ample grass verges
for well over a mile and a half until the gated road down to
Houlsyke is reached. Here strike up to the right on a green path
which unfortunately fades rapidly, but not, at least, until the
ornaments of Danby Beacon are visible directly up the sloping
moor. Keeping left of a row of grouse butts, the road atop the
Beacon will soon be gained.

Leave Danby Beacon by the unsurfaced road to the
right, this splendid moorland track very gradually descending
Lealholm Moor until after almost two miles it swings right at a
fork to join the moor road. To return to Lealholm either turn
left down the road, or if tempted by the causeway departing

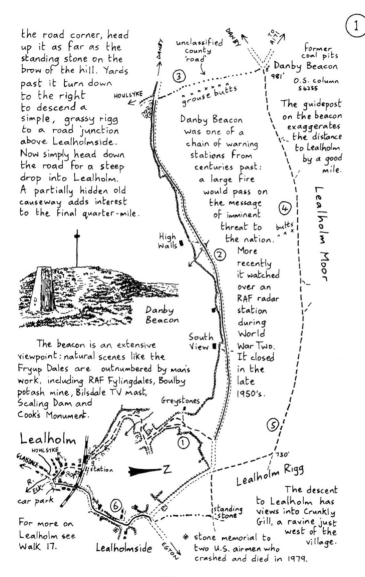

①

the road corner, head up it as far as the standing stone on the brow of the hill. Yards past it turn down to the right to descend a simple, grassy rigg to a road junction above Lealholmside. Now simply head down the road for a steep drop into Lealholm. A partially hidden old causeway adds interest to the final quarter-mile.

unclassified county road

DANBY

TO A171

former coal pits
Danby Beacon
981'
O.S. column S4255

The guidepost on the beacon exaggerates the distance to Lealholm by a good mile.

③ HOULSYKE
××××××× grouse butts

Danby Beacon was one of a chain of warning stations from centuries past: a large fire would pass on the message of imminent threat to the nation. More recently it watched over an RAF radar station during World War Two. It closed in the late 1950's.

Lealholm Moor

④ butts ×××

High Walls

②

Danby Beacon

South View ■

The beacon is an extensive viewpoint: natural scenes like the Fryup Dales are outnumbered by man's work, including RAF Fylingdales, Boulby potash mine, Bilsdale TV mast, Scaling Dam and Cook's Monument.

Greystones

⑤

730'
Lealholm Rigg

The descent to Lealholm has views into Crunkly Gill, a ravine just west of the village.

Lealholm
HOULSYKE
GLAISDALE
station
R. ESK
car park

①

N

For more on Lealholm see Walk 17.

⑥

Lealholmside

EGTON

standing stone

✳ stone memorial to two U.S. airmen who crashed and died in 1979.

(2)

WALK 2

6 miles

MALLYAN SPOUT AND WHEELDALE MOOR

From Goathland

looking south-east

A cracking moorland and beckside walk, even without its two outstanding features

Park in the vicinity of the church at the top of the village, or walk up from the car park in the centre.

Alternative start: the parking area by the road-end near Hunt House

THE WALK

      Leave the road by an iron gate to the right of the Mallyan Hotel, from where a path descends to the trees enclosing West Beck. Take the well-worn path upstream, soon arriving at the Fall of Mallyan Spout on a small tributary. After a scramble over the rocks beneath it continue upstream, the trees thinning out but the beck remaining a constant companion until a road is reached. Turn left up it as far as a sharp left bend and then branch right on a track to an isolated house.

      Head past the house on a splendid green path above the intake wall until arrival at a fence corner. Our continuing path goes straight ahead at this crossroads of green ways, but first a short detour to see Nelly Ayre Foss is well recommended. Turn right with the fence and then downstream a short way to view the falls, reached by a short, steep bank. Steps must now be retraced up this cul-de-sac path to regain the fence corner.

      Back on the main route, turn right here along an inviting path which slants ever so gradually over the low moor to meet up with the Wheeldale road. Turn right along it to a parking area, then double back down a farm road to the right. At the bottom a footbridge leads over Wheeldale Beck, then the path goes downstream a few yards before turning left and rising through two fields to arrive dramatically at the Roman road on the moor edge.

14

2

Head along the Roman road to a stile in an intervening wall, and then on further (ignoring a crossroads with the Lyke Wake Walk) to where a path forks to the left opposite a notice. It descends to recross Wheeldale Beck by means of stepping stones and then swings left to pass by Wheeldale Lodge. From here on it continues as a wide track to Hunt House Farm, whereupon it becomes surfaced.

At this very point branch off half-right up the unpromising, virtually pathless slope, soon entering a thick carpet of bracken. Keen eyes will locate a narrow path up through it, a nick in the skyline above helping to identify its course. At the top of the slope the bracken gives way to a heather plateau, and our way forks left just before a large cairn. The path now contours happily atop a line of modest rock outcrops high above the road, and acts as a boundary between the two distinct forms of vegetation.

This course is maintained for some time until a fork just beyond a graceful cairn. Although the main path will also return safely to the start, the right fork leads us down to a rather surprising feature, a small tarn. A wider path is joined above its right-hand bank, continuing a little past the water before heading over the brow on the left. A gentle descent to Goathland completes the walk, passing the pinfold to return to the very starting point.

Goathland is a wonderful place, a breezy inland resort sat on a green couch amidst the moors. With its heather surround this scattered village's setting positively exudes healthiness, from the solid church of St. Mary down to the deep-set station on the North Yorkshire Moors Railway. In between, the houses and hotels stand back from an extensive green-cum-common, a favourite haunt of the local sheep: note also the causeways. In the depths of winter one can witness - without the crowds - the sword dance team of the Plough Stots performing an ancient custom throughout the village.

The Roman road on Wheeldale Moor is one of the best preserved in the country. About 16 feet wide, it was uncovered at the beginning of the century. Also known as Wade's Causeway, it strikes across the moor in highly impressive fashion.

West Beck is an extremely lively and colourful watercourse formed by the merging of Wheeldale Beck and Wheeldale Gill. Though it contains the attractive if modest Nelly Ayre Foss, it stands only at the foot of the main fall, Mallyan Spout. An innocuous side-stream is the setting for this spectacular mini-series of cataracts. 'Spout' is an apt name, and it is clearly a popular draw for visitors.

From the road to Hunt House the Roman road and track thereto can be picked out quite clearly across the valley.

Wheeldale Lodge, originally a shooting lodge, has been a youth hostel for several decades now.

LWW = Lyke Wake Walk

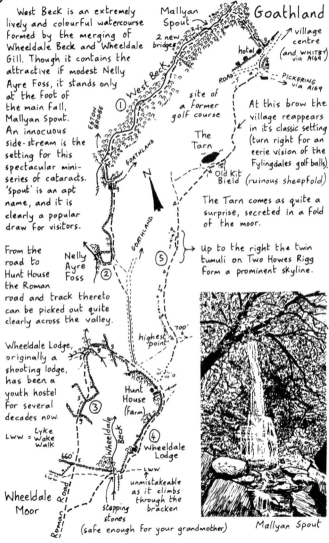

Goathland

Mallyan Spout

2 new bridges

West Beck

Eston Bridge

hotel

village centre (and WHITBY via A169)

ROAD

PICKERING via A169

site of a former golf course

GOATHLAND

The Tarn

Old Kit Bield (ruinous sheepfold)

At this brow the village reappears in it's classic setting (turn right for an eerie vision of the Fylingdales golf balls).

The Tarn comes as quite a surprise, secreted in a fold of the moor.

N

Nelly Ayre Foss

②

GOATHLAND

⑤

Up to the right the twin tumuli on Two Howes Rigg form a prominent skyline.

highest point

700'

③

Hunt House (farm)

④ Wheeldale Lodge

Wheeldale Beck

660'

Roman Road

LWW

Wheeldale Moor

stepping stones

(safe enough for your grandmother)

unmistakeable as it climbs through the bracken

Mallyan Spout

WALK 3

7¼ miles

BAYSDALE AND HOGRAH MOORS

from Westerdale

A walk into lonely Baysdale taking advantage of glorious moorland tracks.

looking south-west

Park on the roadside in the centre of the village.

THE WALK

From the village centre take the lane by the 'phone box towards Westerdale Hall youth hostel. Remain on it past the hostel grounds, and just beyond take a stile to descend the field on the right. Through a gate at the bottom go right to follow the Esk a few yards down to a footbridge. On the other side turn left and accompany the fence rising away from the river. After a gate strike up the centre of two fields to the prominent Brown House. Skirt the left of the house by stile and gate, and climb the sunken fieldside path behind. A stile gives access to the moor, with an unfenced road joined by rising left with a wall. Go right for 200 yards to the brow of the road, then take a path rising back to the left. Known as Skinner Howe Cross Road, it rises steadily over the moor before undulating along Baysdale's southerly slopes.

The second beck encountered is Great Hograh Beck, which is crossed by a tiny arched bridge. A path rises half-right away from it to join a track which is followed right to leave the moor at a gate. Just beyond is Low House, and from its yard go straight across to a stile into a plantation. Continue along its bottom to leave by a gate at the end, then cross to a stile in a short section of facing wall. Two field-tops are taken in to reach Thorntree House, whose triangular pasture is left by a gate at the very top. A forest track climbs away through the trees to a gate back onto the moor.

Turn left with the fence to avoid the grouse butts

17

and thus reach a gate in the rising wall. From it climb to the right on a thin path rising uniformly to a substantial cairn on Holiday Hill. The path continues across the moor to return us to the bridge over Great Hograh Beck. Outward steps are retraced back to the John Breckon Road, and as there is no right of way to short-cut the impending dog-leg, go left to the Kildale road and then double back. The road descends to the Esk before climbing back into the village.

A more interesting conclusion can be implemented by vacating the road half-way down to the river in favour of a stile on the left where a fence replaces a wall. Descend a long narrow pasture parallel with the road to arrive at Hunter's Sty Bridge, across which the road is rejoined to climb up to the village.

Baysdale is a secluded valley which prefers to remain locked away from the outside world. Very much twentieth century however is the afforestation of the upper dale. In the valley bottom below Thorntree House is Baysdale Abbey, a farm on the site of a twelfth century Cistercian nunnery. On crossing Hograh Moors we see Kildale Moor rising across Baysdale Beck: all this country is hallowed grouse-shooting terrain.

The vicinity of Great Hograh Beck is a charming place to linger. The tiny arched bridge is dated 1938, and marks the upper limit of the trees.

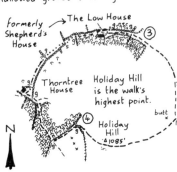

The cairn above Great Hograh Beck incorporates a recent memorial tablet, and also serves as a splendid viewpoint. Across Baysdale to the north-west the unmistakeable tip of Roseberry Topping sneaks into the picture in a scene which is devoted very largely to moorland. A thoughtfully chosen site.

The cairn above Great Hograh Beck

Westerdale Hall youth hostel

Westerdale is the first Esk-side village, and gives its name to this upper reach in preference to 'Eskdale'. Its buildings cling to a street rising from the river to the moor. Of interest in this backwater are the church, the hall, and a monument in the garden of a house. The Victorian hall was built as a shooting lodge, but for many decades has served as a youth hostel of real character.

Hunter's Sty Bridge, bypassed by the road now, is a centuries-old packhorse bridge. On the descent to it note the faint traces of the old causeway that once served with it.

KILDALE ↑

Little Hograh Moor

Little Hograh

John Breckon Road

⑥   750'

butts

① Brown House

N

⑦ cricket pitch

Hunter's Sty Bridge
R. Esk

R. Esk   Hall

CASTLETON

ROSEDALE HEAD

Hall Farm

Westerdale

The return path over the moor has extensive views down towards Castleton and distant Eskdale.

From John Breckon Road are views of Castleton Rigg and Westerdale's valley.

Just off-route is Westerdale Mill, a former mill and cut

WALK 4

4¾ miles

HAYBURN WYKE AND NEWLANDS DALE

from Cloughton

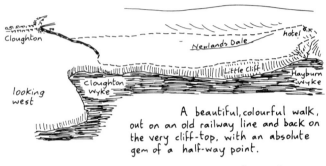

Cloughton

Newlands Dale

hotel

Little Cliff

Cloughton Wyke

Hayburn Wyke

looking west

A beautiful, colourful walk, out on an old railway line and back on the very cliff-top, with an absolute gem of a half-way point.

Start from the crossroads at the northern end of the village, where the Ravenscar road leaves the Scarborough-Whitby road and a minor road heads down to the coast. Park either on the main street towards the village, or down the minor road ('to Court Green Close'): there is room for several cars opposite the farm just beyond the houses. An alternative would be to drive the half-mile to the road's abrupt end above the cliffs, with a small parking area.

THE WALK

From the above-mentioned crossroads turn down the minor road to a bridge over the old railway line, and take a gate on the left to head north along the track-bed. A good mile and a half later the track is dissected by a road, and here leave the line to follow the road down to end at the Hayburn Wyke Hotel just below.

Keep left of the hotel to a gate, and on again left of some barns to a stile. Head off on a sketchy track which goes right after a tree, dropping to a stile into the woods of the nature reserve. Within yards take the broad path left down through trees, ignoring a branch left further down before, nearer the bottom, meeting a branch climbing right: this is the path we shall take after descending the last few yards to the wooden footbridge over Hayburn Beck. Just before the bridge a path goes right to gain the shore and a close-up of the waterfall. Returning to the aforementioned junction (Cleveland

Way sign in evidence) climb steeply through the trees, passing two right forks before reaching a stile at the very top of the woods. At once we are also on the cliff-tops, and now follow this well-defined course for another mile and a half to Cloughton Wyke. Our route vacates the coast path before it rounds the inlet by taking an equally clear path forking right, just beyond the path down to the shore. At the top of a short pull a road-end is met, and is followed back over the old railway to the start of the walk.

The climb up the wood has a seat with a spectacular view. Take care!

Hayburn Wyke is a highlight of the coast, a delightful wooded valley bringing its greenery to the very shore. Rugged cliffs rise on both sides, while a waterfall spills forth onto the rock-strewn beach itself.

NB: this retrospective view of Hayburn Wyke is not to be missed.

Hayburn Wyke once had its own railway station (note the remains of the platform).

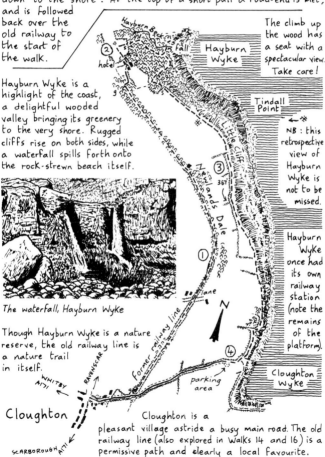

The waterfall, Hayburn Wyke

Though Hayburn Wyke is a nature reserve, the old railway line is a nature trail in itself.

Cloughton

Cloughton is a pleasant village astride a busy main road. The old railway line (also explored in Walks 14 and 16) is a permissive path and clearly a local favourite.

Map labels: Hayburn Beck, fall, hotel, Hayburn Wyke, ② , Tindall Point, Little Cliff, Newlands Dale, ③ 367, ① , lane, N, Former railway line, WHITBY A171, RAVENSCAR, ④ , parking area, Cloughton Wyke, SCARBOROUGH A171

(5)

WALK 5

6 miles

BECK HOLE AND THOMASON FOSS

from Grosmont

A circuit of the Esk's main tributary, visiting a beautifully located village and waterfall

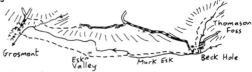

looking
east

Grosmont   Esk   Murk Esk   Beck Hole
              Valley   Thomason
                                             Foss

Use either of Grosmont's
two car parks (one National Park, one Moors Railway)

THE WALK

From the level crossing in the village centre take the footpath alongside the up-line 'to Loco shed and Goathland. After crossing the beck far below it rises left past the school and church. From a gate at the top take a path right, and after rising out of the trees to a seat with a view, take a path through a gate on the left. It soon drops through some trees, above the Loco shed and then runs close to the railway line before a wicket-gate gives access to a wide track running parallel to the line.

When the railway parts company we continue on what is the track-bed of the former line, passing through the tiny settlement of Esk Valley and into trees. The Murk Esk is crossed by a footbridge, and after a long embankment the way enters a wood to run alongside the river. After a stile into a clearing, fork right to a large stone bridge, then turn left (without crossing the river) to tread the old line again. Soon the track meets a beck: do not be tempted by its stepping stones but turn left up the beckside to emerge into the centre of Beck Hole.

From this very point the detour to Thomason Foss presents itself. This cul-de-sac footpath commences straight over the road, rising towards the railway line and then falling steeply to the beck before ending, very firmly, in the rocky amphitheatre containing the waterfall.

Steps must now be retraced into Beck Hole before turning right to negotiate the steep road past the green and high over the railway line. On turning left the road soon eases as it runs along the bottom of a moor. Only yards beyond a phone box fork left on a minor road, passing through a farm and then on quite a way before reaching Dale End Farm. Here the road becomes rougher, going behind the buildings and then steeply down above a beck to enter a wood. After the trees have disappeared from our left side, a footpath sign on the right is the key to a path through the trees to a footbridge over the beck, then rising to emerge onto the Whitby road as it leaves Grosmont. Turn left to drop steeply back into the village.

Thomason
Foss

The preserved railway between Grosmont and Pickering was originally part of the Whitby and Pickering Railway, which was completed in 1836 as a horse-drawn tramway. A decade later it was improved to take steam locomotives: the tunnel near the start of our walk overshadows the initial tramway tunnel. Apart from a short break the walk to Beck Hole traces this old route. At Beck Hole a treacherously steep incline operated to rise up to Goathland, but its deficiencies resulted in the construction of a deviation line between Grosmont and Goathland.

Opened in 1865 the replacement track improved the gradient to 1 in 49 by beginning its climb much earlier. Though the 'new' line parts company on leaving Grosmont, we see it again above Beck Hole. En route to Thomason Foss we climb to the lineside, briefly, and here a good comparison can be drawn, for the original route is still down by the river. Thus Beck Hole became an early station casualty, though a plaque on its site records a temporary reawakening in 1908. A century later the entire Grosmont-Pickering section was closed, to then be saved by enthusiasts and re-opened, initially as far as Goathland, in 1973.

Beck Hole itself exudes character, a sleepy hamlet in an enchanting setting: lazily smoking chimneys on red roofs, ducks, sheep, a quoits (Eskdale's 'own' game) pitch on the green and a novel inn sign, an oil painting. And it is in a hole, too!

23

Grosmont is a pleasant village at the foot of several steep roads. In the 19th century it was dominated by ironstone mining. Today the railway forms the main feature, for here the Esk Valley line meets the privately-run North Yorkshire Moors Railway, and each has a station. This is the northern terminus of the Moors Railway, which cuts through the heart of the moors to run the 18 miles to Pickering. Regular steam-hauled services operate during the season.

Grosmont (then Grosmond) was the location of an abbey of the 'rare' Grantimontine Order. This minor establishment was dissolved in 1536, and Priory Farm now occupies the site. Earlier still, a Roman fort existed in the neighbourhood.

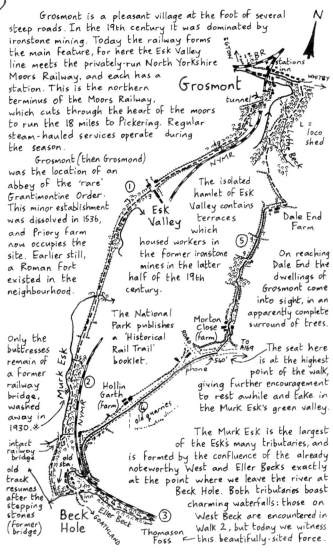

N

Grosmont

L = loco shed

WHITBY

tunnel

The isolated hamlet of Esk Valley contains terraces which housed workers in the former ironstone mines in the latter half of the 19th century.

Dale End Farm

On reaching Dale End the dwellings of Grosmont come into sight, in an apparently complete surround of trees.

The National Park publishes a 'Historical Rail Trail' booklet.

Only the buttresses remain of a former railway bridge, washed away in 1930.*

intact railway bridge
old track resumes after the stepping stones (former bridge)

Beck Hole

Morton Close (farm)

To A169

540'

phone

Hollin Garth (farm)

old quarries

Murk Esk

NYMR

old sta.

inn

Eller Beck GOATHLAND

Thomason Foss

The seat here is at the highest point of the walk, giving further encouragement to rest awhile and take in the Murk Esk's green valley.

The Murk Esk is the largest of the Esk's many tributaries, and is formed by the confluence of the already noteworthy West and Eller Becks exactly at the point where we leave the river at Beck Hole. Both tributaries boast charming waterfalls: those on West Beck are encountered in Walk 2, but today we witness this beautifully-sited Force.

WALK 6

DANBY RIGG AND DANBY DALE

7 miles

from Ainthorpe

A typical moorland ridge walk precedes a potter round the unspoilt Danby Dale.

Park either in the vicinity of the inn, or a little higher up the road where it reaches the open moor between two tennis courts.

THE WALK

From the inn follow the road uphill onto the moor, and just beyond the tennis courts take a bridleway directly up the moor. It rises to a gate in a fence then eases out to cross the broad ridge to its steep eastern fall into Little Fryup Dale. To be correct the right-of-way now descends to the junction of roads, turns right for about 250 yards then climbs back up to the edge of the ridge. It is easy to follow and demands little extra effort, but most walkers will no doubt be tempted by the more obvious path along the very ridge-edge.

The point where these two paths cross is marked by a second cairn, some 200 yards along from a row of shooting butts. Now follow the narrow path which turns away from the edge to cross the broad ridge top, soon arriving at a similar situation on its western edge, now overlooking Danby Dale. A sunken path zig-zags down to a gate then drops down a bracken field to another gate above Eastcliffe Farm. Just above the buildings take a stile on the left, crossing a field to two more stiles and then a gate to pass in between the buildings of Roger House. The access road is now accompanied down to meet the valley road.

For a visit to Botton village turn immediately left up Hall Drive leading directly to it. Back on the 'main' road turn down to cross Danby Beck before a steep pull up the opposite slope. On reaching a farm on the left, turn off right along an enclosed farm road. This ceases at the second of two neighbouring farms: simply continue in a straight line along an enclosed way, then across a field-top, a field-bottom and onto another enclosed track to a farm. Now on a surfaced farm road we pass a fourth farm before descending to cross Danby Beck again. A steep climb up the other side brings us to a stile on the right, from where a field is crossed to reach Danby church.

Leave the church by its drive, turning left and on through a staggered junction, and then continue ahead on a straight, level road down-dale. Within five minutes leave the road by a track branching right, directly across a field. It rises through another field, becomes briefly enclosed and then swings left to approach Rowantree farm. Continue on between its buildings to accompany its access road out onto the moor road above Ainthorpe. The village is just down to the left.

Between Stormy Hall and Danby Church we encounter the route of a former limers' road, in use up to the last century. Its purpose, along with that of several other such roads, was to bring lime from quarries on the southern moors for agricultural use in and around Eskdale. In some cases coal would be traded in return.

Botton village is a rather special settlement. In 1955 a charitable trust set up a working community for mentally handicapped adults, and now, more than 30 years on, around 300 people are involved. The scheme has non-disabled working alongside in an effort to create a normal environment. Around the dale head are several farms, while in and around the centre can be found dairy, bakery, post office, coffee shop and even a bookshop!

Our route between the farms yields fine views down the dale to Castleton and also across to the church. Castleton Rigg is up to our left.

Little Fryup Head from Danby Rigg

The lonely church of St. Hilda has a 15th century tower and looks up to the high moors so loved by its famous incumbent, Canon J. C. Atkinson. Vicar here for 53 years, his deep knowledge of local life and history led to his classic work 'Forty Years in a Moorland Parish'. He was laid to rest here in 1900.

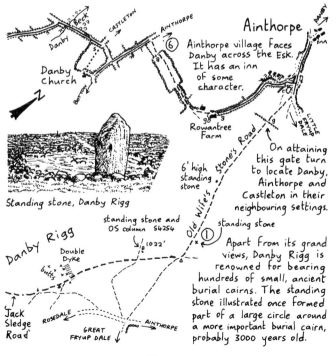

Danby Church

Ainthorpe

Ainthorpe village faces Danby across the Esk. It has an inn of some character.

Rowantree Farm

On attaining this gate turn to locate Danby, Ainthorpe and Castleton in their neighbouring settings.

6' high standing stone

Stone's Road

Old Wife's

Standing stone, Danby Rigg

standing stone

① standing stone

Danby Rigg

standing stone and OS column S4254
↓ 1022'

Double Dyke

butts

Jack Sledge Road

ROSEDALE

GREAT FRYUP DALE ↓

AINTHORPE

Apart from its grand views, Danby Rigg is renowned for bearing hundreds of small, ancient burial cairns. The standing stone illustrated once formed part of a large circle around a more important burial cairn, probably 3000 years old.

WALK 7

7½ miles

| PORT MULGRAVE AND BORROWBY DALE |

from Staithes

looking south-west

A popular
coastal walk and a
lesser Known hinterland

Use Staithes' main car park

Alternative start: Runswick Bay car park (for a finish along the cliffs)

| THE WALK |

From the car park turn down the main street to the seafront, and depart the village by the steep Church Lane rising behind the Cod and Lobster inn. At its demise a path takes over the climb, going left at a fork to rise to a farm. A clear path heads across the fields before a short pull up to the cliff-top. The path then runs along the cliffs to soon arrive at Port Mulgrave. Here a detour can be made from where the road turns inland, by taking a path from the gate on the left to descend steeply to the tiny harbour.

From the road end, meanwhile, the cliff path continues around the next headland to then turn inland at a stile to arrive at Runswick Bank Top. Here is an optional detour down the cul-de-sac road to the lower village and the shore. From Bank Top the walk turns inland for good, along the road (with its own adjacent footpath) into Hinderwell.

Turn right along the length of the village until just prior to reaching the road to Port Mulgrave by the parish church. Turn down Porret Lane on the left, and by a former Methodist chapel a guidepost points the way along a narrow path by the front of a terrace. This unlikely-looking way sneaks between the houses at the end to debouch onto a lane, crossing straight over and down another narrow way onto a wide track by a house. Keep on until it swings sharply left, then continue straight on down the fieldside to a stile. A path then materialises to drop half-right to another stile and down to a footbridge over Dales Beck.

A stepped path climbs out of the trees: turn right along the field-edge to re-enter the trees at a sharp bend, and go left along a good path. Running along a distinct ridge in the wood, our path merges with another before leaving the trees. Go across the field and continue on to where a track materialises to descend to a farm bridge. The wide track heading away leads into Dalehouse: turn right up the lane onto the main road, right along that and then first left to re-enter Staithes.

Looking to Kettle Ness From Port Mulgrave

Staithes is a fishing port and a former smuggling centre, and despite tourism it remains a delightful place. A large portion stands up by the Whitby - Middlesbrough road, but the crowd-puller is the lower half by the seafront. Here many buildings cluster into little space, either perched above the deep-cut beck or facing the small harbour. It is the sea that is linked with every aspect of Staithes life. The boats sheltering in the mouth of the beck will be seen, and the Mission Church of St. Peter the Fisherman. Staithes has its share of savage storms, and the seafront Cod and Lobster inn has often been a prime target.

Here James Cook earned his first wages serving in a shop, and a story relates how a south-sea coin he took in inspired him to go forth on his life of adventure. The beck now forms the county boundary, and the north bank, known as Cowbar, marks the beginning of Cleveland county.

Hinderwell is a sizeable village clinging doggedly to the main road through it. The most interesting corner of this linear settlement is found at its northern extremity, in the vicinity of the church. St. Hilda's dates from 1773 and stands island-like, surrounded by a triangle of roads. Inside its churchyard can be found the ancient well, said to have been blessed by Hilda, who was Abbess of Whitby in the 7th century – hence the name of the village. It is thought she kept a cell here in which to pray, away from the distractions of the abbey. An annual show is held in the village in August.

On climbing above Staithes the impressive Cowbar Nab is dwarfed by the immense bulk of Boulby Cliff.

Note the novel pictorial sign at the Staithes lane end, and on descending the lane note the buttresses of a once mighty railway viaduct across Staithes Beck.

The hamlet of Dalehouse hides just beneath the busy main road, and in its environs several substantial becks merge to form the short-lived Staithes Beck.

One mile to the west hovers the National Park showpiece, Boulby potash mine, a modern addition whose thousands of feet of depth would be fine if they didn't require the appalling sight on the surface!

Penny Steel · Jet Wyke · Old Nab · Cowbar Nab · Staithes Beck · Fullwood Farm · ① · car park · Staithes · Beacon Hill 378' × · site of the Hinderwell Beacon · LOFTUS A174 · WHITBY A174 · Dalehouse · SCALING · inn · ⑦ · ROXBY · BORROWBY · caravans · Dales Beck · Borrowby Dale · STAITHES A174 · PORT MULGRAVE · Hinderwell · ⑥ · N

After leaving Hinderwell look back to see the church's setting, and further north Boulby's cliff somewhat obstructed by its mine.

Port Mulgrave is a curious but nevertheless very interesting place, known chiefly for it's mini-harbour which is separated from the hamlet by 300 feet of rough slopes. Though visible from the cliff-top path, the harbour is worth scrambling down to, wooden steps having been introduced to arrest the path's erosion. The tiny port was constructed in the mid-19th century, when the mining of iron-ore was in full swing. The ore came through a mile-long tunnel to be shipped up the coast to the large ironworks. The bricked-up entrance still adorns the cliff, and is indeed visible from the path.

The scene today is of near-dereliction, with the short harbour walls well past their best. Half a dozen or so local boats still make use of the shelter. Back on the cliff-top, note the long terrace of former miners' cottages just inland.

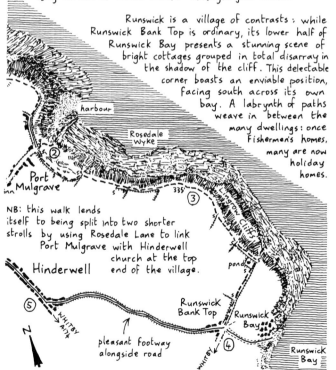

Runswick is a village of contrasts: while Runswick Bank Top is ordinary, its lower half of Runswick Bay presents a stunning scene of bright cottages grouped in total disarray in the shadow of the cliff. This delectable corner boasts an enviable position, facing south across its own bay. A labrynth of paths weave in between the many dwellings: once fishermen's homes, many are now holiday homes.

harbour

Rosedale Wyke

②

Port Mulgrave
inn

335'

③

NB: this walk lends itself to being split into two shorter strolls by using Rosedale Lane to link Port Mulgrave with Hinderwell church at the top end of the village.

Hinderwell

⑤

WHITBY WAY

pond

pleasant footway alongside road

Runswick Bank Top

Runswick Bay

④

WHITBY WAY

Runswick Bay

N

WALK 8

5¼ miles

from May Beck

looking south-west

Attractive woodland and a famous waterfall

May Beck car park
(Forestry Commission) is signposted off the B1416 at Red Gate between
Sneaton and its junction with the A171 north of the Flask Inn.

Alternative starts: Falling Foss or Littlebeck (village hall) car parks

THE WALK

Begin on a narrow footpath climbing the bracken slope
behind the car park, almost immediately crossing the farm track
to Old May Beck before continuing up. Soon the path bears right
to rise to a stile, then runs along to the right above the trees.
Keep with a fence on the left, and at a fork take the narrow path
sloping gently right: it runs on to another stile to enter the
woods proper, then descends pleasantly to a wide farm track.

Falling Foss is just down to the right, but for now go
up the track to a group of barns (formerly Foss Farm). A little past
them, take a gate on the right to follow a lesser track down to a
bridge: just beyond is Leas Beck Farm. A stile on the left is the key
to its drive climbing the field and heading directly away, becoming
surfaced at Intake Farm to descend unfailingly into Littlebeck.

Turn right over the bridge in Littlebeck and up the
road as far as the second bend, where a wicket-gate leads into
the woods on the right. A good path heads upstream, becoming
temporarily diverted from Little Beck by a lovely waterfall on a
tributary. Later, at a fork, climb to the right to round a spoil
heap and continue on, soon rising steeply to the Hermitage.

Leave the Hermitage by the upper path which soon
has a wall for company, first on the left, then the right. When the
path forks up to the left take the right-hand path to descend
towards Falling Foss, soon arriving at a well-sited viewpoint above the
fall. From the nearby footbridge take the path up to the access road,
crossing it to stepping stones to follow the beck upstream again. The
path soon improves to lead back to May Beck Bridge and car park.

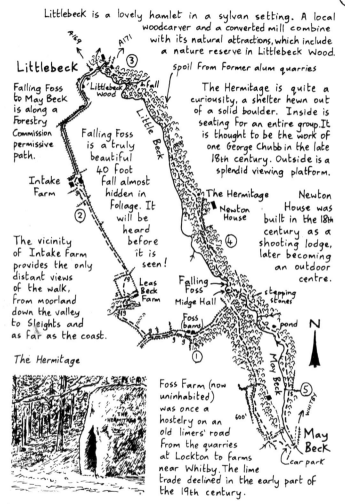

Littlebeck is a lovely hamlet in a sylvan setting. A local woodcarver and a converted mill combine with its natural attractions, which include a nature reserve in Littlebeck Wood.

Littlebeck

A169
A171
③

Littlebeck Wood
+ fall
spoil from former alum quarries

Little Beck

Falling Foss to May Beck is along a Forestry Commission permissive path.

Falling Foss is a truly beautiful 40 foot fall almost hidden in foliage. It will be heard before it is seen!

The Hermitage is quite a curiosity, a shelter hewn out of a solid boulder. Inside is seating for an entire group. It is thought to be the work of one George Chubb in the late 18th century. Outside is a splendid viewing platform.

Intake Farm
②

The Hermitage
Newton House
④

Newton House was built in the 18th century as a shooting lodge, later becoming an outdoor centre.

The vicinity of Intake Farm provides the only distant views of the walk, from moorland down the valley to Sleights and as far as the coast.

Leas Beck Farm

Falling Foss
Midge Hall
Foss barns
①

stepping stones
pond
N

May Beck

The Hermitage

Foss Farm (now uninhabited) was once a hostelry on an old limers' road from the quarries at Lockton to farms near Whitby. The lime trade declined in the early part of the 19th century.

600'
⑤
WHITBY
May Beck
car park

May Beck car park has opened up the higher woods to visitors. A nature trail (leaflet available) to Falling Foss (Forestry Commission permissive path) is complemented by a trail upstream (National Park booklet).

Falling Foss

WALK 9 | MULGRAVE WOODS AND SANDSEND NESS

7 miles   from Sandsend

NB: See note on page 37 re access to the woods

looking west

A vivid
contrast
between
glorious
woodland
and a
former industrial coastline

Use either of the two handily
placed car parks

THE WALK

        From the main car park at the north end of the
village cross the bridge over Sandsend Beck and follow the
road along the front. When it swings in to cross East Row Beck,
don't cross it but enter the rough car park, taking a gate
at its far end into Mulgrave Woods (N.B. unless otherwise said,
the tracks used in the woods are wide and well-surfaced).
        A drive heads through the trees, passing a timber
yard and then on for a good mile. A little beyond a wooden
hut is a fork, the left arm going down to a bridge across
East Row Beck: remain on the top path, as they rejoin further
on to continue to a fork just before a tunnel underneath
the ridge on the right. From here a short detour to visit the
ruined castle can be made. Just prior to the fork a narrow
path rises up to the right to a green track. Follow it up to
the left – over the tunnel, in fact – to soon arrive below the
castle remains. They can best be seen by following the track
round to the rear.
        Having retraced steps to the tunnel entrance, pass
under it and head away along the drive, crossing a bridge
over Sandsend Beck before a long steady rise to eventually
arrive at a T-junction on the edge of the wood. To the left
is a private drive up to the 'modern' Mulgrave Castle, so
turn right to cross a large field to emerge onto Lythe Bank
at a lodge.
        Turn up the hill on a raised footpath as far as

Lythe's isolated church, and just past it take a track right. This access road is followed to Deepgrove Farm. Take the gate on the right of the buildings and then turn behind them to the field corner. Continue along the next field to a stile into wooded Overdale, descending steeply through trees to a footbridge and then reversing the process up the other side. From the stile head away to the left with the hedge to a sudden and dramatic halt at the cliff-top above Loop Wyke.

Turn right along the cliffs to the next stile and then turn inland with the wall to return to leafy Overdale. An extremely steep drop on wooden steps ensues, but at least a re-ascent is not required for at the bottom we join the course of the former coastal railway. The line returns us unfailingly to Sandsend, a flight of steps descending to the car park just prior to reaching the old station building.

Mulgrave Castle ruins

Sandsend is well named, for here the long stretch of sandy beach from Whitby comes to an abrupt halt as the rocky shoreline takes over. Strictly speaking this is two settlements, with East Row forming the other half. Each sits at the foot of its own beck (which run parallel) and from their respective bridges we can look inland to two equally charming scenes of beckside cottages and woods.

A century ago Sandsend was known for two main things, its alum quarries and a railway line, though the two were never of use to each other. When the line arrived in 1883 the alum industry had ceased, but between Sandsend and the Ness evidence abounds, even to the extent of the headland having its appearance totally altered. A nature trail (National Park booklet) now explores this area, making use of the line which ceased to be an exhilarating journey in 1958.

Sandsend Ness from Sandsend

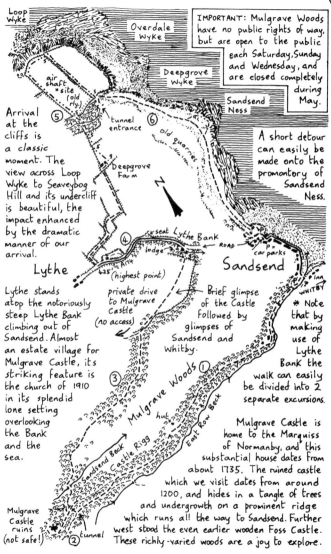

Loop Wyke

Overdale Wyke

Deepgrove Wyke

Sandsend Ness

air shaft *site (old rly.)

⑤

tunnel entrance

⑥ old quarries

IMPORTANT: Mulgrave Woods have no public rights of way, but are open to the public each Saturday, Sunday and Wednesday, and are closed completely during May.

Arrival at the cliffs is a *classic* moment. The view across Loop Wyke to Seaveybog Hill and its undercliff is beautiful, the impact enhanced by the dramatic manner of our arrival.

A short detour can easily be made onto the promontory of Sandsend Ness.

Deepgrove Farm

N

seat Lythe Bank

④ ROAD

lodge

425 Arb (highest point)

Lythe

private drive to Mulgrave Castle (no access)

Brief glimpse of the Castle followed by glimpses of Sandsend and Whitby.

Sandsend

P
car parks

Inn
WHITBY

Lythe stands atop the notoriously steep Lythe Bank climbing out of Sandsend. Almost an estate village for Mulgrave Castle, its striking feature is the church of 1910 in its splendid lone setting overlooking the Bank and the sea.

* Note that by making use of Lythe Bank the walk can easily be divided into 2 separate excursions.

③

① Mulgrave Woods

hut

East Row Beck

Sandsend Beck

Castle Rigg

Mulgrave Castle ruins (not safe!)

② tunnel

Mulgrave Castle is home to the Marquiss of Normanby, and this substantial house dates from about 1735. The ruined castle which we visit dates from around 1200, and hides in a tangle of trees and undergrowth on a prominent ridge which runs all the way to Sandsend. Further west stood the even earlier wooden Foss Castle. These richly-varied woods are a joy to explore.

WALK 10

BEGGAR'S BRIDGE AND ARNECLIFF WOOD

3¾ miles

from Egton Bridge

A modest stroll through charming mid-Eskdale

looking north

Use the small car-park by the school

Limber Hill

Glaisdale

East Arncliff Wood

River Esk

Egton Bridge

Alternative start: by the roadside at or just above Beggar's Bridge, Glaisdale

THE WALK

From the road junction on the north side of the bridge take the branch towards Glaisdale. After a spell by the river it rises under a railway bridge and past Broom Farm. A short way above it take a stile on the left to run above the top of a wood. When the fence parts company continue above the trees, and bear half-left to cross a tiny stream. Rise up the steep slope behind, aiming for a stile in the plantation at the top.

A path runs through the trees, soon emerging to head away by a hedge. In the field beyond, an access track to the mast on the left is followed towards the farm ahead. Don't enter its yard however, but turn down the narrowing pasture on the left to a gate at the end, then double back right to a gate onto a hairpin bend at the top of Limber Hill. Turn down its steep slope to run alongside the Esk at the bottom to arrive at the environs of Beggar's Bridge.

Having no doubt used this famous structure to cross the river, pass under the imposing railway bridge then leave the road immediately by a footbridge over Glaisdale Beck to enter East Arncliff Wood. The path climbs steeply then descends to the river, soon climbing again to then traverse the wood in undulating fashion before emerging out onto a quiet road.

Turn down the road all the way to a T-junction at the edge of Egton Bridge, just beyond a hotel. Leave the road at this junction by some steps down to the river, leading to some sturdy stepping stones : once across, rise between some houses onto the road by which we began. If averse to running water, remain on the road to finish by crossing Egton Bridge.

Beggar's Bridge is a true work of art, a graceful arched structure high above the Esk. The present bridge dates from the early 1600's and served the packhorse era. It is said to have originally been constructed by Tom Ferris, a local lad who became Mayor of Hull. Restored now, and a tourist attraction, it is incongruously sandwiched between an overshadowing railway bridge and a modern featureless road bridge.

For a note on Egton Bridge, see Walk 18

The path in East Arncliff Wood

The walk through East Arncliff Wood is one of great variety, with a riverside section soon giving way to a path high in the trees: the drop to the river is extremely steep. Occasional views of river and railway can be had. A lengthy stretch of the path is along a paved pannier way from the packhorse days. This walk is dominated by trees, the early riverside section from Egton Bridge being especially attractive.

Limber Hill is a good vantage point for the scattered village of Glaisdale. Prominent are the rows of ex-miners' cottages.

The stepping stones over the Esk at Egton Bridge break their journey on a wooded islet, giving a misleading impression of having reached the opposite bank already!

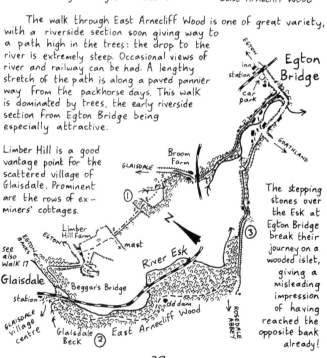

WALK 11

5¾ miles

DANBY CASTLE AND CLITHERBECK

From Danby

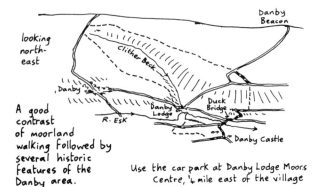

looking north-east

A good contrast of moorland walking followed by several historic features of the Danby area.

Use the car park at Danby Lodge Moors Centre, ¼ mile east of the village

THE WALK

Leave the car park by turning right along the road towards Danby, almost at once reaching a junction behind Danby Lodge. Leave the road on this bend by a gate straight ahead to climb through a small wood. On leaving the top end of the wood follow a wall away, the track soon becoming sketchy as a right fork heads down to Clither Beck. Our way remains with the wall until a gate admits to bracken pasture on the left.

Climb with the wall on the left to the top of a minor rigg, then strike up to a wall-corner on the right. A little further up, the wall bends sharply right and a wider track known as the Lord's Turnpike is met: turn right onto it but then be sure to opt for the left-hand of the three branches into which it immediately divides. This broad green way crosses the open moor to eventually merge with the road out of Danby.

Turn right over the bridge and along the road for 150 yards, then head right along a farm road. When it turns down to Clitherbeck farm keep straight on along the track by the fence. At a corner 150 yards (again) beyond a beck crossing the track forks: take the left arm running fairly level across the moor. The site of the Castleton pits is passed before eventually joining another moor road at a junction.

Cross straight over and down the narrow strip of

tarmac to another junction, again going straight across and down an enclosed track onto the next lane. Go right along it to drop down to the valley road just beyond a railway bridge. Go right again for a short distance then take a minor road to the left to cross Duck Bridge. Turn left along the lane behind it to climb steeply to a junction. Danby Castle is just yards to the left and worth a closer look from the roadside.

Returning to the junction take the level road along to the left as far as a gate on the right, from where a field is descended until level with Castle Houses Farm. Now strike left to a stile and continue down to a gate in the corner, then head directly away up the next field to its far side, turning left to leave it at the corner. A right turn then leads back onto a road.

Head right along the road and a short distance past Kadelands House take a stile on the left to head down to cross the railway line. Continue away from it to a footbridge over the Esk, just beyond which is Danby Lodge and the start of the walk.

Duck Bridge, Danby

Danby Castle dates from the fourteenth century and was the fortified home of the Latimer family, though its best known resident was reputed to have been Catherine Parr, one of Henry's half-dozen. The not insignificant remains are intertwined with farm buildings still very much in use, and although not open to the public, it is well seen from the road: the substantial southern wall looks over an extensive panorama of mid-Eskdale. A room is used for the meetings of Danby Court Leet (see over).

Duck Bridge is another shapely 14th century structure, a former packhorse bridge over the Esk. It has a fine view of the castle it was probably constructed to serve.

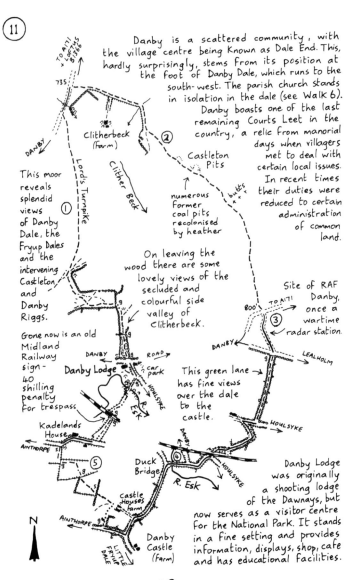

Danby is a scattered community, with the village centre being known as Dale End. This, hardly surprisingly, stems from its position at the foot of Danby Dale, which runs to the south-west. The parish church stands in isolation in the dale (see Walk 6).

Danby boasts one of the last remaining Courts Leet in the country, a relic from manorial days when villagers met to deal with certain local issues.

In recent times their duties were reduced to certain administration of common land.

TO A171 + LOFTUS B1366

735

Clitherbeck (Farm)

②

DANBY

Lord's Turnpike

Clither Beck

Castleton Pits

numerous former coal pits recolonised by heather

butts

This moor reveals splendid views of Danby Dale, the Fryup Dales and the intervening Castleton and Danby Riggs.

①

On leaving the wood there are some lovely views of the secluded and colourful side valley of Clitherbeck.

Site of RAF Danby, once a wartime radar station.

800

TO A171

③

DANBY

LEALHOLM

Gone now is an old Midland Railway sign – 40 shilling penalty for trespass

DANBY ROAD

Danby Lodge

car park

HOULSYKE

R. Esk

This green lane has fine views over the dale to the castle.

HOULSYKE

Kadelands House

AINTHORPE STN

⑤

DANBY

Duck Bridge

④

R. Esk

HOULSYKE

Danby Lodge was originally a shooting lodge of the Dawnays, but now serves as a visitor centre for the National Park. It stands in a fine setting and provides information, displays, shop, cafe and has educational facilities.

N

Castle Houses farm

AINTHORPE

Danby Castle (Farm)

LITTLE FRYUP DALE

WALK 12
6¼ miles

THE KETTLENESS COASTLINE
from Goldsborough

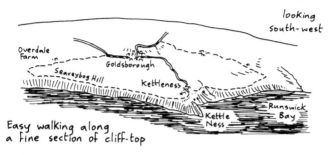

looking
south-west

Overdale Farm
Goldsborough
Seaveybog Hill
Kettleness
Kettle Ness
Runswick Bay

Easy walking along
a fine section of cliff-top

Park in the tiny village centre. Alternative start: Kettleness

THE WALK

From the central T-junction set off along the 'no through road' towards Kettleness, but at the first bend take a stile on the left to climb up a field-edge onto another road. Go right only as far as the farm road branching off, and turn right along it through the fields to Brockrigg Farm. Continue straight on (right of the main buildings) and the track keeps going through two more fields before swinging right to reach Claymoor Farm.

Keep right of the farm and maintain the same course to descend two pathless fields to a bridge over the line of a former railway. Cross the bridge and turn right until the cliff top comes in close, then join the coastal path which heads along the cliffs to Kettleness.

After the farm buildings on the right take the left-hand of two tracks forking left to resume the cliff-top walk. The path continues its course for almost two miles, the briefest of breaks from the cliff-top coming when the path rises a little sketchily to the left of an old tunnel entrance on the way to the high point of Seaveybog Hill.

The cliffs are finally vacated after a sharp little swing left to a stile just beyond a collapsed wall. The stile bears an acorn symbol, and on its other side a yellow waymark. From it go right to a stile by a gate: a track heads right to Overdale Farm's access track, up it to join a road, from where we turn right for the village.

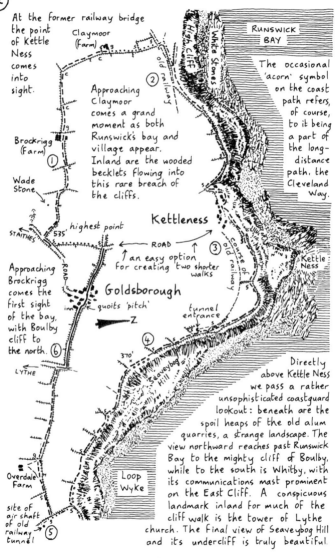

At the former railway bridge the point of Kettle Ness comes into sight.

Claymoor (Farm)

RUNSWICK BAY

The occasional 'acorn' symbol on the coast path refers, of course, to it being a part of the long-distance path, the Cleveland Way.

Approaching Claymoor comes a grand moment as both Runswick's bay and village appear. Inland are the wooded becklets flowing into this rare breach of the cliffs.

High Cliff

White Stones

② old railway

Brockrigg (Farm) ①

Wade Stone

STAITHES

535' highest point

Kettleness

ROAD ③

↑ an easy option for creating two shorter walks

course of old railway

Kettle Ness

Approaching Brockrigg comes the first sight of the bay, with Boulby cliff to the north. ⑥

ROAD

Goldsborough

inn quoits 'pitch'

Z

tunnel entrance

LYTHE

④

370'

Seaveybog Hill

Loop Wyke

Overdale Farm

site of air shaft of old railway tunnel ⑤

Directly above Kettle Ness we pass a rather unsophisticated coastguard lookout: beneath are the spoil heaps of the old alum quarries, a strange landscape. The view northward reaches past Runswick Bay to the mighty cliff of Boulby, while to the south is Whitby, with its communications mast prominent on the East Cliff. A conspicuous landmark inland for much of the cliff walk is the tower of Lythe church. The final view of Seaveybog Hill and its undercliff is truly beautiful.

Kettle Ness from High Cliff

Kettleness is a tiny community that was once larger, for more than a century and a half ago a previous hamlet fell victim to the North Sea. Midway between this settlement and Goldsborough is the site of a Roman signal station, and a more modern Coastguard station still exists here. The Roman one is just off the road, and its outline can still be clearly discerned.

Goldsborough is another tiny settlement, only half a mile from the sea but 500 windswept feet above it. Farming is its business, and a little inn slots rather unexpectedly into the cluster of buildings.

Just above the hamlet on our outward route we pass Wade's Stone, in curious isolation in the centre of a large field. It has a twin a mile to the south, and legend has it that a giant Saxon king of that name is buried between the two.

The spectacular old coastal railway was opened from Loftus to Whitby in 1883, and in a short section between Kettleness and Sandsend tunnels it ran across the cliff of Seaveybog Hill. It closed in 1958.

Wade's Stone

The old tunnel entrance, Kettleness

45

WALK 13

6 miles

AROUND COMMONDALE

from Castleton

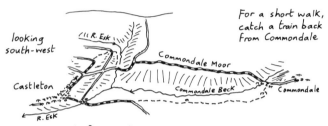

looking south-west

R. Esk

Commondale Moor

Castleton

Commondale Beck

Commondale

R. Esk

For a short walk, catch a train back from Commondale

An easy circuit of an early tributary of the Esk. Little routefinding, and varied views of the upper dale.

Park either on the village main street or down by the road junction before the river and railway station.

THE WALK

From the village centre junction near the Downe Arms take the road leading down to the railway station, then continue up the slope beyond and onto the moor. Leave the road at a bend right by forking left at a wide track along a wall-side. This bridleway to Commondale lives up to its promise, remaining broad throughout as it undulates above the intake wall and the nearby railway line. Eventually a small wood is entered and the track becomes enclosed to drop down to the road passing by Commondale station.

The village centre is just two minutes along to the right, but our route takes us down the road over the beck and under the railway before climbing the hill beyond. Remain on this moor road with its accommodating verges all the way to a T-junction, turning left to descend to cross Dibble Bridge over the river Esk. Here leave the road to follow the river upstream, a thin path at once materialising to rise gradually through bracken above the Esk. At a fence-corner a wider green way takes over to lead up onto an unfenced road into Westerdale.

Just to the left an inviting green path rises from the road, soon forking before a gate: take the left one to remain on the moor, still rising before running on to meet a road junction. Go left along this quiet road (good verges again) which soon returns us to the top end of Castleton's main street.

46

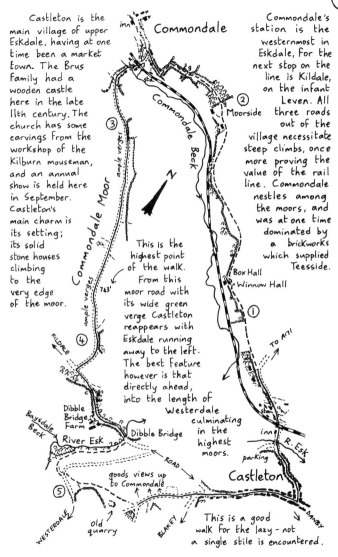

Castleton is the main village of upper Eskdale, having at one time been a market town. The Brus family had a wooden castle here in the late 11th century. The church has some carvings from the workshop of the Kilburn mouseman, and an annual show is held here in September. Castleton's main charm is its setting; its solid stone houses climbing to the very edge of the moor.

Commondale's station is the westernmost in Eskdale, for the next stop on the line is Kildale, on the infant Leven. All three roads out of the village necessitate steep climbs, once more proving the value of the rail line. Commondale nestles among the moors, and was at one time dominated by a brickworks which supplied Teesside.

This is the highest point of the walk. From this moor road with its wide green verge Castleton reappears with Eskdale running away to the left. The best feature however is that directly ahead, into the length of Westerdale culminating in the highest moors.

Commondale

Moorside

Commondale Beck

Commondale Moor

ample verges

743'

Box Hall

Winnow Hall

TO AM

KILDALE

Dibble Bridge Farm

Baysdale Beck

River Esk

Dibble Bridge

ROAD

good views up to Commondale

WESTERDALE

old quarry

BLAKEY

inn

parking

Castleton

R. Esk

DANBY

inn

This is a good walk for the lazy - not a single stile is encountered.

WALK 14

5¼ miles

BOGGLE HOLE AND STOUPE BROW

From Robin Hood's Bay

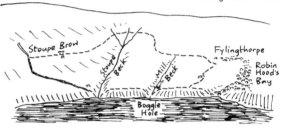

looking south-west

A good exploration of the Robin Hood's Bay area, combining a defunct railway line with an invigorating coastal walk.

Start from the seashore at the foot of the main street, using the cliff-top car park at the top (the nearest that vehicles are allowed)

THE WALK

From the very foot of the main street walk back only a few yards and head along the tiny Albion Road. Stone steps are followed by more recent ones as the cliff-top is quickly gained. A stile on the right, however, soon takes us away from the coast along a fenced path to Farsyde Farm. Passing right of the farm its access road is joined and followed away to the site of a one-time railway bridge just after a right fork. Climb up to the left to gain the old line, which is now our route for about 2½ miles as far as the Stoupe Brow road.

On the way the journey is interrupted only once, by a minor road. A big curve then ensues to Browside Farm, and it is immediately after the next overhead bridge that we vacate the line to join a road. It descends steeply towards Stoupe Bank Farm, from where a modern flagged path leads down to a footbridge over Stoupe Beck. If the tide is safely out, there is the option of an easy walk back to Robin Hood's Bay along the shore. Otherwise, climb the steep slope opposite, the ensuing level walk soon being broken by a drop to Boggle Hole. Another steep climb from the footbridge precedes another level walk, rejoining the outward route to finish the walk.

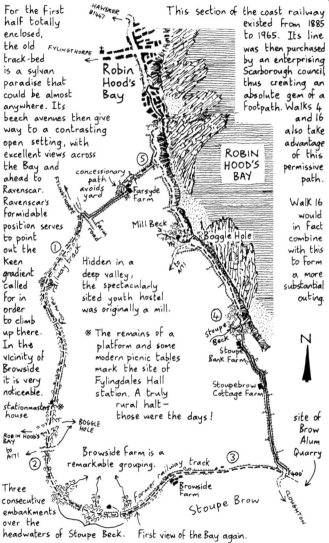

For the first half totally enclosed, the old track-bed is a sylvan paradise that could be almost anywhere. Its beech avenues then give way to a contrasting open setting, with excellent views across the Bay and ahead to Ravenscar. Ravenscar's formidable position serves to point out the keen gradient called for in order to climb up there. In the vicinity of Browside it is very noticeable.

This section of the coast railway existed from 1885 to 1965. Its line was then purchased by an enterprising Scarborough council, thus creating an absolute gem of a footpath. Walks 4 and 16 also take advantage of this permissive path.

Walk 16 would in fact combine with this to form a more substantial outing.

Hidden in a deep valley, the spectacularly sited youth hostel was originally a mill.

※ The remains of a platform and some modern picnic tables mark the site of Fylingdales Hall station. A truly rural halt — those were the days!

Browside farm is a remarkable grouping.

Three consecutive embankments over the headwaters of Stoupe Beck. First view of the Bay again.

stationmasters house

ROBIN HOOD'S BAY to A171

BOGGLE HOLE

site of Brow Alum Quarry

Stoupe Brow

49

Robin Hood's Bay, with the advantages of both an exciting name and an even better location, will be found in many people's list of favourite places. Once the preserve of fishermen and smugglers, it is now very much part of the tourist itinerary.

Known in the locality simply as Bay Town, it consists of a chaotic tumble of red-roofed buildings squeezed into only a narrow gap between cliffs. From the modern extension of housing at the cliff-top, the steep main street plunges down to the very shore. On each side are irregular groupings of shops and dwellings, with short, narrow passageways linking the near-hidden doorsteps.

King Street

The village has suffered badly from storms, and the Bay Hotel once had a ship driven into it by the savage weather: a modern sea-wall now ensures a little more safety. The bay itself is generally regarded as a geologist's mecca, with fossils in abundance and a spectacular sweep of flat scars curving round the bay almost like a natural extension of the tide. At low tide this can be well appraised during the return walk.

Boggle
Hole
Youth
Hostel

50

WALK 15

7 miles

from Glaisdale

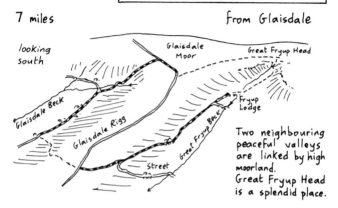

Two neighbouring peaceful valleys are linked by high moorland. Great Fryup Head is a splendid place.

Park by the roadside at Applegarth (identifiable by the adjacent isolated 'phone box) 2¼ miles up the valley of Glaisdale from the road junction in Glaisdale village below the Mitre public house.

THE WALK

Begin by walking back along the road in the direction of the village, but after a couple of minutes leave by a gate on the left to enter a narrow strip of moorland reaching down to the very roadside. A green track rises through the bracken, climbing steeply to the right before easing out on the edge of Glaisdale Rigg. Continue across the moor to soon meet the broad unsurfaced road running along the rigg.

Cross straight over to a very thin but equally clear path, with the guidepost directly ahead beckons us unfailingly to a moor road junction. Again cross straight over and along the minor road which almost immediately begins a steep descent into Great Fryup Dale. Shortly after becoming enclosed at a cattle-grid the road forks: take the left arm which drops down through the fields to a farming hamlet. Keep straight on up-dale, continuing on the 'no through road' when the valley road turns right.

Our road ends at Fryup Lodge, but keep straight on the track between the buildings to a bridge over the beck. It continues upstream through several fields to arrive at the barns of Dale Head. Go right of the buildings and just beyond a tiny stream turn right up a sunken path. Recross the stream to a collapsed wall at the top, behind which a stile in a fence leaves us on a level path. Go left along it as it keeps just above the intake wall, and when the wall drops away the path heads on through bracken to a gate in an intervening wall.

Now in the amphitheatre of Great Fryup Head, the path drops down to cross the beck in front before climbing the slope behind. A smaller beck is then crossed and followed upstream before the path begins its short, steep climb out of the valley head. Above some outcrops the gradient eases and the path rises gently across the moor to meet a wide path at a large cairn.

Turn left along this well-used way around the top of the valley head to eventually join a moor road. Go right along it as far as a junction, then turn down the steep little road back into the valley of Glaisdale. From the junction at the bottom, the start point is only five minutes along to the left.

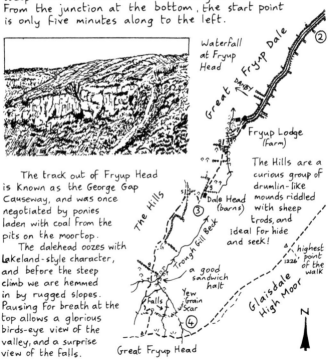

The track out of Fryup Head is known as the George Gap Causeway, and was once negotiated by ponies laden with coal from the pits on the moortop.

The dalehead oozes with Lakeland-style character, and before the steep climb we are hemmed in by rugged slopes. Pausing for breath at the top allows a glorious birds-eye view of the valley, and a surprise view of the falls.

Waterfall at Fryup Head

Great Fryup Dale

DANBY

Fryup Lodge (farm)

The Hills

The Hills are a curious group of drumlin-like mounds riddled with sheep trods, and ideal for hide and seek!

Dale Head (barns)

③

Trough Gill Beck

a good sandwich halt

Yew Grain Scar

Falls

④

Great Fryup Head

highest point of the walk 1226'

Glaisdale High Moor

N

Considering the nature of the terrain and the distance, the actual climbing involved is restricted to two steep but short sections.

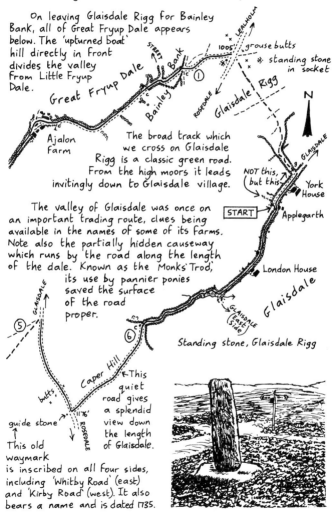

On leaving Glaisdale Rigg for Bainley Bank, all of Great Fryup Dale appears below. The 'upturned boat' hill directly in front divides the valley from Little Fryup Dale.

Great Fryup Dale

STREET

Bainley Bank

①

ROSEDALE

1005' grouse butts

LEALHOLM

x x standing stone
   in socket

Glaisdale Rigg

N

Ajalon Farm

The broad track which we cross on Glaisdale Rigg is a classic green road. From the high moors it leads invitingly down to Glaisdale village.

GLAISDALE

NOT this,
but this

York House

START

Applegarth

The valley of Glaisdale was once on an important trading route, clues being available in the names of some of its farms. Note also the partially hidden causeway which runs by the road along the length of the dale. Known as the 'Monks' Trod,' its use by pannier ponies saved the surface of the road proper.

London House

Glaisdale

GLAISDALE (east side)

GLAISDALE

⑤

⑥

Caper Hill

← This quiet road gives a splendid view down the length of Glaisdale.

butts

guide stone →

1176'

ROSEDALE

Standing stone, Glaisdale Rigg

This old waymark is inscribed on all four sides, including 'Whitby Road' (east) and 'Kirby Road' (west). It also bears a name and is dated 1735.

WALK 16

5¼ miles

THE ENVIRONS OF RAVENSCAR

from Ravenscar

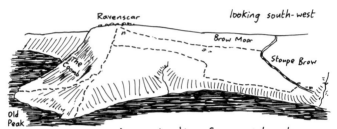

An exploration of many interesting features, including cliff-top, the former railway line, old alum quarries and the fascinating undercliff and shore beneath breezy Ravenscar. Very easy walking apart from the (optional) steeper descent to the shore.

Start from the National Trust Information Centre, using the linear parking alongside the 'main' road descending to it.

THE WALK

Set off by the wide track between the information centre and the hotel to descend to the golf course. At a sharp bend in the track leave it (temporarily) by a footpath continuing down to the cliff-top. The cliff is reached at a National Trust sign, and if a potter round the shore and undercliff appeals then descend the well-worn path with care (see also the notes by the map).

On returning to the cliff-top National Trust sign, go back up to the bend in the track and turn right on it, crossing the golf-course and continuing on over two cattle-grids to merge with another track coming in from the left. At a stile soon after becoming enclosed, a path branches right to run quickly down to the clifftop.

The path now heads clearly above the cliffs until a narrow enclosed way channels us onto the by-now adjacent road at Stoupebrow Cottage Farm. Turn left along this road and then steeply up until it bridges the old railway line. Here join the line and follow it left almost all the way back to Ravenscar. Just short of the finish we are diverted onto a parallel path (the line enters a tunnel) to rise back up to the information centre.

Ravenscar is unlike any of the other coastal villages, being perched a breezy 600 feet up on the cliff-tops. For this reason it failed dismally as a planned holiday venue: in the 1890's work began on establishing a resort, but its hostile location caused its abandonment after thirty years. Some signs of the intended street layout are still in evidence.

On a sunny day however, this is a wonderful place to imbibe the bracing sea air. A geological trail (National Park booklet) explores the old alum quarries and the rocky foreshore. The longer path down the undercliff has bracken clinging on virtually to the very shore, and is well worth the effort involved.

Of further interest is a National Trust information centre and the end of the Lyke Wake Walk.

The views are magnificent throughout, almost always looking north across the bay to Robin Hood's Bay, with – if the tide is out – its classic scar formations.

Here are two major features of the area, both long disused but still very much in evidence. The quarrying had ceased over a decade before the railway arrived in 1885, but in 1965 this also disappeared, becoming a permissive path. Note the relatively steep gradient in the short pull to Ravenscar.

Stoupe Beck

Stoupe Bank Farm

Stoupebrow Cottage Farm

③ bunker

Flat Scars

NB: if the tide is safely out, the shoreline could be followed to Stoupe Beck.

400'

CLOUGHTON

site of the Former Brow Alum Quarry

Miller's Nab

④

Stoupe Brow Farm

course of former railway

site of Peak Alum Quarry

②

golf course ①

Low Nook

Old Peak

The Coomb

⑤   625'

hotel

Ravenscar

CLOUGHTON

The start of this walk also happens to be its highest point.

WALK 17

5½ miles

GLAISDALE AND THE RIVER ESK

from Lealholm

An easy walk by lanes, pastures, moorland, village, wood and then
the Esk's environs.
Real variety!

Start from the
village centre
car park

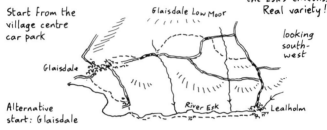

Alternative
start: Glaisdale

THE WALK

From the car park cross the bridge and ascend the
Rosedale road (some verges) for almost a mile, passing branches
to left and right and a footpath sign left before arriving at
a bridleway sign. Cross to the gate on the left then aim half
right to a gate in the bottom corner of the field. From the little
footbridge below it, rise to the right-hand of two gates to follow
two field-tops before emerging onto the moor.
Within 50 yards a road is reached: turn left along
it until almost enclosed by walls, then escape along a track up
to the right. It soon swings left down to a house, then continues
sketchily down by a fence. Take a gate on the left to descend
a long, narrow bracken pasture to a gate, continuing down now
on a clear track to join an access track, and a little to the
left, a road. Turn right along it to enter the top of Glaisdale
village. At the hilltop, when the road becomes enclosed again,
it can be neatly escaped by taking the track right but then
leaving it immediately by a stile on the left. The left-hand
field boundary is then followed away through several fields
to emerge between houses onto a road. Turn left to rejoin the
road through the village.
Descend the road through Glaisdale to a crossroads
by the Mitre then take the narrow road down to the left. Just
beyond a sharp bend take a gate on the left into Millers
Wood: a drive descends to a house whereupon a footpath takes
over to rise through the wood to a stile, continuing on to leave

56

the trees at the next stile. The path then runs along the top of a field to another stile, before heading half-left to a stile to enter the confines of Thorneywaite. Keep to the right of the buildings to a stile onto a minor road and then set off down it, continuing straight down when it departs by turning right, to descend a steep track to the river Esk.

Cross the footbridge and take the track away to the left, vacating it just prior to surmounting the railway line by a narrow path through the bracken on the left. Briefly sandwiched in trees between river and railway, we soon emerge to shadow the wooded riverbank to Underpark Farm. From the gate into its yard keep left of the buildings and then head out along the enclosed access road to the left. Remaining near the river this well-surfaced way leads unfailingly back into Lealholm, emerging adjacent to the car park.

The bridge

The Esk at Lealholm

The stepping stones

Lealholm is an immensely attractive village in a setting to match, and as such is a popular haunt of visitors. This compact settlement is ruled by the Esk: a nice stone bridge links the houses and is supplemented by well-used stepping stones a little further upstream. Alongside bridge and river is a spacious green on which Eskdale's 'national game' of quoits is played. Two adjacent churches compete on the climb to the ubiquitous station, with ubiquitous moors only a little further up.

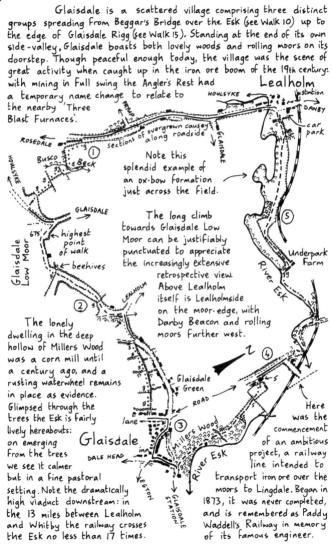

Glaisdale is a scattered village comprising three distinct groups spreading from Beggar's Bridge over the Esk (see Walk 10) up to the edge of Glaisdale Rigg (see Walk 15). Standing at the end of its own side-valley, Glaisdale boasts both lovely woods and rolling moors on its doorstep. Though peaceful enough today, the village was the scene of great activity when caught up in the iron ore boom of the 19th century: with mining in full swing the Angler's Rest had a temporary name change to relate to the nearby 'Three Blast Furnaces'.

Lealholm

HOULSYKE — station — DANBY — car park

ROSEDALE

sections of overgrown causey along roadside

GLAISDALE

HOULSYKE

BUSCO — ① — Beck

Note this splendid example of an ox-bow formation just across the field.

GLAISDALE

675 — highest point of walk

beehives

Glaisdale Low Moor

⑤

Underpark Farm

River Esk

The long climb towards Glaisdale Low Moor can be justifiably punctuated to appreciate the increasingly extensive retrospective view. Above Lealholm itself is Lealholmside on the moor-edge, with Danby Beacon and rolling moors further west.

LEALHOLM

②

The lonely dwelling in the deep hollow of Millers Wood was a corn mill until a century ago, and a rusting waterwheel remains in place as evidence. Glimpsed through the trees the Esk is fairly lively hereabouts: on emerging from the trees we see it calmer but in a fine pastoral setting. Note the dramatically high viaduct downstream: in the 13 miles between Lealholm and Whitby the railway crosses the Esk no less than 17 times.

Glaisdale Green

ROAD

④

lane

③ — Millers Wood

Glaisdale

DALE HEAD — inn

EGTON

GLAISDALE STATION

River Esk

Here was the commencement of an ambitious project, a railway line intended to transport iron ore over the moors to Lingdale. Began in 1873, it was never completed, and is remembered as Paddy Waddell's Railway in memory of its famous engineer.

WALK 18

ALONG THE ESK VALLEY

5¾ miles

from Sleights

A linear walk linking two historic routes - a toll road and a pannier way - by use of the Esk Valley railway

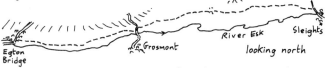

looking north

Although the walk can be started at either end, the recommendation is to use the car park by the railway station at Sleights, then catch the train the short journey to Egton Bridge to commence the return walk to Sleights.

THE WALK

Leave the road in Egton Bridge by the enclosed way between the bridge and the church, signposted 'Egton Estates private road'. This former toll road runs down-dale to emerge onto a road on the edge of Grosmont, the village being just to the right across the bridge. Our route, however, turns left a few yards before branching right on a surfaced road 'to Priory Park'. When the road turns sharp left continue straight ahead on the farm road to Grosmont Farm. It passes between the buildings and heads away again to rise to Fotherleys Farm. Without entering its confines take a small gate on the left.

A paved path now rises through Cote Bank Wood to emerge at a gate, then runs to the right along two field-bottoms to join the drive to Newbiggin Hall. Turn along to the right, passing alongside the buildings and then on through two field-bottoms to enter a wood. On leaving it several more field-sides are crossed before entering another wood. Here a path slopes down to the right (temporarily leaving the paved way) to join a farm road. Cross to a path opposite and then almost at once fork left down to a footbridge.

Rise up the field behind, passing beneath a wood and across more fields to another farm lane. Turn right to its demise at Thistle Grove then go right just before the farmyard to cross more fields and rise onto a drive. Turn down it to the right to run along to the Whitby - Pickering road. One final right turn leads across the bridge and back to the station.

59

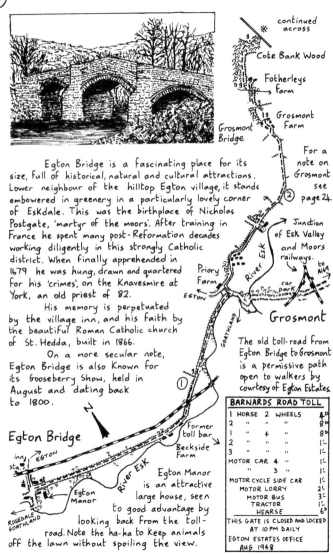

continued
across

Cote Bank Wood

Fotherleys
Farm

Grosmont
Farm

Grosmont
Bridge

For a
note on
Grosmont
see
page 24

Junction
of Esk Valley
and Moors
railways.

to A169

car
park

EGTON

Priory
Farm

Grosmont

GOATHLAND

Egton Bridge is a fascinating place for its size, full of historical, natural and cultural attractions. Lower neighbour of the hilltop Egton village, it stands embowered in greenery in a particularly lovely corner of Eskdale. This was the birthplace of Nicholas Postgate, 'martyr of the moors'. After training in France he spent many post-Reformation decades working diligently in this strongly Catholic district. When finally apprehended in 1679 he was hung, drawn and quartered for his 'crimes', on the Knavesmire at York, an old priest of 82.

His memory is perpetuated by the village inn, and his faith by the beautiful Roman Catholic church of St. Hedda, built in 1866.

On a more secular note, Egton Bridge is also known for its Gooseberry Show, held in August and dating back to 1800.

The old toll-road from Egton Bridge to Grosmont is a permissive path open to walkers by courtesy of Egton Estates

Egton Bridge

inn
sta.
EGTON

Egton
Manor

ROSEDALE
GOATHLAND

River Esk

Former
toll bar

Beckside
Farm

Egton Manor is an attractive large house, seen to good advantage by looking back from the toll-road. Note the ha-ha to keep animals off the lawn without spoiling the view.

BARNARDS ROAD TOLL			
1 HORSE 2 WHEELS			4ᵈ
2 "	"	"	8ᵈ
1 "	4	"	8ᵈ
2 "	"	"	1ˢ
3 "	"	"	1ˢ
MOTOR CAR 4	"		1ˢ
"	3	"	1ˢ
MOTOR CYCLE SIDE CAR			1ˢ
MOTOR LORRY			2ˢ
MOTOR BUS			3ˢ
TRACTOR			1ˢ
HEARSE			6ᵈ

THIS GATE IS CLOSED AND LOCKED
AT 10 PM DAILY
EGTON ESTATES OFFICE
AUG 1948

Sleights is a growing village which is virtually surrounded by the National Park boundary. Its sprawl of suburban avenues provide a dormitory for Whitby, only 3 miles down-river. The main street climbs relentlessly from the Esk's bank, at one time being on the salters' route from Whitby to Pickering. The church dates from the 12th century, while on the river is an old corn mill dam. The Esk is renowned hereabouts as a great salmon river.

The Esk Valley railway line is a blast from the past, a rare survivor from the scything down of most of its fellow country cousins. The line runs from Middlesbrough to Whitby, and a journey along its entire length is well repaid. There is a good regular service enabling this walk to be planned with ease (but no Sunday service in winter). Times can be obtained from sources on page 9, or many places locally.

Between Fotherleys and Woodlands, the majority of the walk is along a paved pannier way, a real gem. In use in packhorse days, it is thought that monks bound for Whitby Abbey may have come this way.

Newbiggin Hall is a most impressive farmhouse dating from the 17th century.

Sleights

On joining this drive two great northern saints are recalled: Hilda at a former school (now Woodlands nursing home) and Oswald at the pastoral centre with its fine frontage.

Before and after Thistle Grove there are good open views of the Esk, with Sleights Moor rising sharply behind.

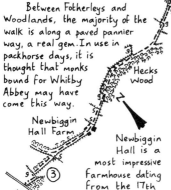

The pannier way near Thistle Grove, looking back to Sleights Moor

LOG OF THE WALKS

These two pages provide an opportunity to maintain
a permanent record of the walks completed

WALK	DATE	TIME Start	TIME Finish	WEATHER	COMMENTS
1					
2					
3					
4					
5					
6					
7					
8					

| WALK | DATE | TIME | | WEATHER | COMMENTS |
		Start	Finish		
9					
10					
11					
12					
13					
14					
15					
16					
17					
18					

KEY TO THE MAP SYMBOLS

Direction of north

Scale
2½ inches = 1 mile (approx.)

Route — — — clear — — — · — · — · sketchy · — · · · · · · · · · · no path

Route on public road — — — unenclosed wall Fence/hedge

③ Miles from start

Railway line

Buildings

Church

Cairns
summit other

Abbreviations
g – gate
s – stile
c – cattle-grid

Crags

Loose rock /scree

Marsh

Trees

river or beck → bridge rocky shore
steep coastal slopes and cliffs North Sea
sand and shingle